CLOTHES & CRAFTS IN THE
MIDDLE AGES

Imogen Dawson

A ZOË BOOK

A ZOË BOOK

© 1997 Zoë Books Limited

Devised and produced by
Zoë Books Limited
15 Worthy Lane
Winchester
Hampshire SO23 7AB
England

First published in Great Britain in 1997 by
Zoë Books Limited
15 Worthy Lane
Winchester
Hampshire SO23 7AB

A record of the CIP data is available from the British Library.

ISBN 1 86173 003 9

Printed in Belgium by Proost N.V.
Editor: Kath Davies
Design & Production: Sterling Associates
Illustrations: Virginia Gray

Author's note

The period that historians call the Middle Ages overlaps with the period known as the Renaissance. For a greater understanding of historical continuity and development, some examples and references to crafts, clothes and festivals in this book fall outside the period, which historians define as the Middle Ages.

Photographic acknowledgments

The publishers wish to acknowledge, with thanks, the following photographic sources:

DDA Photo Library / Thyssen-Bornemisza Museum, Madrid 19br; C.M Dixon 14, 15b / The British Library 9t/ The British Museum, London 13tr / Victoria & Albert Museum, London 17t, 19bl, 21t / Künsthistorisches Museum, Vienna 20t / Palazzo Vecchio, Florence 22t; e.t.archive 11tl, 15t, 17b, 25t & b / Prado Museum, Madrid title page, 7tl, 10t / Victoria & Albert Museum, London 3, 8b, 21b / Royal Chapel, Granada 4t / Hamburg Staatsarchiv 5t / The Louvre, Paris 5b / The British Library, London 6t / Torre Aquila Trento 6b, 16t & bl, 18c / University Library, Heidelberg 7tr, 24t / Biblioteca Estense, Modena 7b, 18b, 24b / Correr Museum, Venice 8t / Musée de Cluny, Paris 9b / Suermondt Museum, Aachen 10b / Museo delgi Argenti, Pitti Palace, Florence 11tc / Real Collegiata San Isidoro, Leon 11b / Bibliotheque Nationale, Paris 12t / Archaeological Museum Cividale Friuli 13tl / Palazzo Pubblico, Siena 16br / Musée Conde Chantilly 18t / British Museum, London 19t / Bargello Museum, Florence 20b / Stadtmuseum Trier (Salomon Collection) 22b / Palazzo Giuntini di Valfonda/Venturi 23t / Sir John Soane's Museum, London 23b; Mansell Collection 13b; Tony Morrison 12b.

Cover: e.t.archive / Bargello Museum, Florence, top right / Diocesan Museum, Mantua, top left / Biblioteca Estense, Modena, bottom left; C.M.Dixon / Victoria & Albert Museum, London, centre; DDA Photo Library / Thyssen-Bornemisza Museum, Madrid, bottom right.

The publishers have made every effort to trace the copyright holders, but if they have inadvertently overlooked any, they will be pleased to make the necessary arrangement at the first opportunity.

CONTENTS

INTRODUCTION

The period of history in Europe that we call the Middle Ages lasted for more than 1000 years, from the collapse of the Roman Empire in AD 476. Before Christopher Columbus arrived in America in 1492, Europeans believed that the world stretched only from western Europe to India and China in the East.

There were far fewer people living in Europe in the Middle Ages than there are today. Most people lived in the countryside and worked on the land. People made their clothes and crafts from local materials such as wool, leather, wood, clay and iron.

Most people followed the **Christian** religion. The Church was very rich and powerful in the Middle Ages. The head of

▲ King Ferdinand and Queen Isabella of Spain were rich and powerful rulers. They paid for Christopher Columbus's voyages to America. The gold and craft goods he brought back were claimed by them.

The Black Death

In the 1300s about a third of all people in Europe died from a disease called the plague, or the **Black Death**.

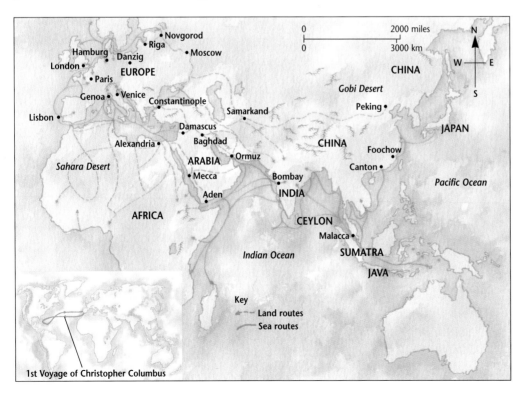

Key
- - - Land routes
— Sea routes

1st Voyage of Christopher Columbus

◀ Traders, or **merchants**, travelled great distances to buy and sell goods. They sailed along the rivers of Europe, or round its coast, and later to North and South America. Some merchants travelled overland to India and China. They brought back goods such as **silk** and **spices**. They carried the goods on pack animals such as donkeys and camels.

paid craftworkers to make new works in these styles. Rebirth of ideas from ancient Greece and Rome happened at this time.

▲ This drawing of the port of Hamburg in Germany was made in 1497. Hamburg was a busy trading city. You can see the merchants dressed in rich clothes, watching their ships being loaded with goods.

the Church, the **Pope**, made the religious laws which everyone, including rulers, had to obey. Rich **nobles** and merchants gave land and money to the Church. Craftworkers were paid to make works of art for churches and cathedrals.

Written records, such as the books and maps, made by **monks** and **nuns**, give us information about the Middle Ages. Paintings and drawings from that time show us how people lived and worked and the kinds of clothes that they wore.

The time towards the end of the Middle Ages is called the **Renaissance**, which means 'rebirth'. People became interested in the writings, buildings, paintings and sculptures of ancient Greece and Rome. Rich people brought back ancient works of art from their travels in Europe. They

The Crusades

Between the end of the 1000s and the 1300s, large groups of **knights** and nobles travelled from Europe to the Middle East. They took soldiers with them to fight for the Christian holy places, such as Jerusalem in Palestine. These journeys were called the **Crusades**. The Christian rulers in western Europe thought that the Turks, who followed the religion of **Islam**, should not control the Christian Holy Land.

▼ This detail, from a painting by Frans Francken, shows a range of craft goods. Only the rich could afford to buy such items, which were made by highly skilled craftworkers.

CRAFTS

Most people lived very simply during the Middle Ages. Everyday things were made from local materials. Only rich people could afford to buy materials and craft goods which came from far away.

People used wood and stone to build their houses, and to make furniture. They made jugs and bowls from clay. The **blacksmith** made farm tools, weapons and cooking tools, or utensils, from iron.

Wood

During the Middle Ages, forests covered most of Europe. People used wood for building and to make boats, carts and furniture such as benches, tables and chests. Rich nobles, who lived in castles or **manor** houses, often decorated the walls

The feudal system

During the Middle Ages, the rulers of countries in Europe gave nobles, or lords the rights, or feus, to land. In return the lords promised to support the ruler, and to provide soldiers who would fight for the ruler in battle.

The **peasants** who lived and worked on the land grew food and raised animals. They had to give some of their food to the nobles who owned the land. Many peasants were not free to move to another part of the country. They were 'tied' to the land.

of their homes with wooden panels. In France and in Scotland, craftworkers painted bright pictures on wooden ceiling panels.

Most homes contained a table, benches, beds and chests, and perhaps some stools made of wood. The chest was the most useful piece of furniture. It could be used as a seat, a table, a sideboard or to store things.

Some nobles slept in four-poster beds. These had four carved posts to hold up a frame. Curtains made of heavy material hung from the frame.

◀ This Italian wall painting, or **fresco**, shows life at a manor house in the summer. Many things, including some of the buildings and tools, are made of wood.

▲ There is very little furniture in this room – just a wooden chest and a chair. This picture was painted by Hieronymus Bosch in about 1500.

▶ People in the Middle Ages loved board games. Chess, which is still played today, was very popular. This drawing, made in 1381, comes from a German manuscript. The ruler, Otto IV, is playing a game of chess.

Nobles travelled around to oversee their lands or to follow the **court**. They took furniture and their most valuable possessions with them. These objects had to be made so that they could be carried easily. Craftworkers made chairs and stools that folded up, boxes for jewellery and chests with strong locks and handles for clothes.

Courts

The court was a gathering of noble lords and ladies, and was held wherever the ruler was staying at the time. There were grand feasts at court. The nobles were entertained by singers and musicians, jugglers, poets and storytellers.

◀ Nobles enjoy music and dancing at court in the summer. The ruler sits in the chair on the left.

Cloth

The wool trade was very important in the Middle Ages. Selling wool and woollen cloth brought wealth to merchants and sheep farmers, including many **monasteries**. Some of the most expensive wool came from the Cotswolds area of England. Merchants sold the wool as far away as Italy.

Turning wool into cloth was a long process. Women worked at home, spinning the wool into long thread, using a **spindle** and a **distaff**. They wove the thread into woollen cloth on a **loom**. Then the cloth had to be washed before it was dyed into different colours. People used all kinds of plants and mosses to dye the wool.

Women in poorer families wove cloth for everyday purposes such as clothes and blankets. Women in richer households and in **convents** also embroidered or wove tapestries.

▲ These merchants in Venice, Italy are weighing wool in a basket. The drawing was made in 1380.

◄ This woman spins wool while she is out in the fields. She holds the distaff under her arm and the spindle in her other hand. The drawing was made in France during the late fifteenth century.

▲ This picture, drawn in the late fourteenth century, shows a tapestry being woven on a wooden frame. You can see the criss-cross threads. The weavers often worked from a sketch made by an artist, which was called a cartoon.

Carpets and tapestries

Unlike today, the word 'carpet' was used for all kinds of woven covers and hangings, not just for floor coverings.

The word 'tapestry' comes from the French word '*tapis*' or carpet.

People used carpets to cover walls, to keep out draughts, or to divide rooms.

Some nobles took their carpets and tapestries on their travels. They were easy to roll up and carry around.

Linen

Linen cloth is made from the long, tough stems of a plant called flax. In the Middle Ages, people softened the flax by leaving it to rot for a time. This was called 'retting'. Then they beat the flax with wooden paddles, so that the stems separated into **fibres**. This was very hard work. The strong fibres were spun into linen cloth. If the flax fibres were thin, the cloth was very fine, and if the fibres were thicker, the linen was coarse. Fine linen was very expensive.

▼ This is one of a set of beautiful tapestries known as the 'Lady and the Unicorn'. The tapestries were made in France during the fifteenth century.

From kitchen to table

Kitchen utensils were probably hung from hooks on the kitchen walls. There was usually little furniture in a kitchen, except for a large table and perhaps a wooden chopping block for meat.

Kitchen utensils

The records of a rich merchant in the 1300s list his kitchen utensils:

'...1 great brass bowl; 2 great copper jars for water; 2 iron pots, that hung on a chain above the fire; 1 copper frying pan; 4 other frying pans, 2 spits and a grill; 20 oil-jars; 1 copper pan 'for making black pudding'; 1 big pan for melting lard [animal fat]; 1 sieve and an iron shovel 'for making pills'; 1 sugar barrel; 1 salt box.'

▲ The most elaborate tableware, made of silver and gold, was used at feasts for the rich. This detail is from a painting by two Flemish artists.

In the early Middle Ages, people ate from wooden bowls or platters. They also used slabs of stale bread, called trenchers, as plates. Later on, people used pottery and metal dishes and plates. Pottery was made locally and sold in the markets. In northern Europe, a grey metal called pewter was used to make plates, jugs and dishes.

Pewter is a mixture of tin and small amounts of lead and copper. The pewterer poured the hot metal into **moulds**. When it cooled, it was polished until it shone like silver. Jugs, or flagons, were made in separate pieces. The pewterer joined or

◀ You can see the grey pewter dishes and jugs, as well as pottery on the table in this picture. This painting of *The Last Supper* is by the Dutch artist, Lucas van Leyden.

◀ Pope Clement VII gave this cup to a church in Florence, Italy. It has been carved from a piece of precious stone, called jasper.

Very wealthy people owned gold plates and drinking cups or goblets. Sometimes the tableware was decorated with precious stones, or jewels.

▲ During the Middle Ages more coins were made, or **minted**, and began to be widely used. Before this time, people had exchanged, or bartered, goods. Local rulers had the right to produce their own coins. This coin was minted for the government in Genoa, Italy.

The search for gold

In Europe, the demand for gold to make coins, jewellery and crafts of all kinds was increasing. After Columbus reached America, the search for gold led explorers further into the lands of the Americas. The traders, who were mostly Spanish, melted down craft goods made of gold. Then they sent the gold blocks back to Europe.

soldered the pieces together with hot, melted metal. This made a bridge between the pieces which held them together after the metal cooled and hardened. The best pewterers were so skilled that you could not see the joins. Pewter was cheaper to buy than silver, so it was called 'poor man's silver'.

Fine glass and silver was made in France, Venice and other parts of Italy. The richer the family, the finer its tableware.

▶ Boxes, called reliquaries, were specially made for the Church. They held the remains of a saint, or other holy objects. This reliquary is crafted from gold and enamel. It was made in Spain during the thirteenth century.

Towns and cities

Towns and cities grew in size during the Middle Ages. They were important centres for trade and they also became centres of learning.

Craftworkers such as candlemakers, jewellers and glovemakers made goods in their town workshops. They sold the goods from the front of the workshop or on market stalls. Potters and leatherworkers needed more room for their crafts, so they often worked near the edge of the towns.

Merchants grew more powerful as their trade increased. Nobles and merchants were now able to order and buy crafts which were made for their beauty rather than for everyday use. Life was still hard for poor people. In towns a whole family might live in one room of a house.

◀ Students attend a class at the Sorbonne university in Paris, France, during the sixteenth century.

After the Black Death swept across Europe in the fourteenth century, the craftworkers who did survive were in even greater demand.

One of the earliest and most famous universities in Europe was founded in the city of Bologna, Italy, during the eleventh century. At first universities were places where men studied to become priests, lawyers or doctors.

▲ Many towns still have a guildhall, where guild members met. This one is in Lavenham, England, which was once a rich wool town.

Craft guilds

In the Middle Ages, craft **guilds** were set up in each town. A guild was an organization which made sure that its members were properly trained as **apprentices** and produced high quality goods.

An apprentice spent seven years learning a trade. Boys could become apprentices in most places. In some places girls were apprentices as well, but only in certain trades. Their parents paid for them to live at the home of the craftworker who taught them their skills.

At the end of the seven year apprenticeship, they had to make a special piece called a masterpiece, to show that they were good enough to join the craft guild.

Guilds also set a fair price for their goods. There was a guild for each type of craft, such as goldsmiths or shoemakers.

◀ This book cover is made of silver, **gilded** with a layer of gold, and set with precious stones. The centre panel is carved ivory. It was made for an Italian noble in the eighth century.

▲ These highly decorated pages are from an illuminated manuscript, made in Paris early in the fifteenth century.

Books

Books were written, copied and bound by hand, usually in monasteries or convents. Sometimes it took years to produce one book. Many of these **manuscripts** had brightly coloured pictures of people, animals and flowers, and gold decoration. Often these pictures formed part of the first letter in each section of a book. Manuscripts decorated in this way are called **illuminated** manuscripts.

When printing was invented in the fifteenth century, there were many more books for people to buy and to study. We know that books were precious at this time, because they were mentioned in people's wills. Books were very expensive and beyond the reach of poorer people, who in any case could not read.

William Caxton

William Caxton was an English wool merchant who learned the craft of printing in Germany. In 1476, he set up the first printing press in England. He printed and published all kinds of books in English, from poetry to an illustrated encyclopedia. Caxton also translated histories and religious works into English. On the right is a page from one of his translations, *The lives of the fathers*. It was printed by his assistant in 1495, shortly after Caxton's death.

Important buildings

During the Middle Ages, many of the best craftworkers travelled around Europe to work on important buildings. Palaces and cathedrals were being built from stone and marble. Craftworkers decorated them with stone or wooden carvings, stained glass, and painted pillars and ceilings.

▲ This splendid stained-glass window at Canterbury Cathedral portrays Henry VIII, who became King of England in 1509.

The 'Prentice Pillar'

The 'Prentice Pillar' is in Rosslyn Chapel, near Edinburgh, Scotland. The Chapel was built around 1450. This is the story that is told about it.

An apprentice was given permission to carve the pillar while the master mason was away. When the master returned, he saw that the pillar was so beautifully carved that it outshone all his own work. In a rage, the master hit the apprentice over the head so hard that he killed him. The master was hanged for the murder of the apprentice.

Rich nobles employed craftworkers to decorate their homes with paintings, sculptures and frescoes. In Spain, people put brightly coloured pottery tiles on their floors and walls.

Spanish crafts were influenced by the styles of the **Moors**. These people came from North Africa, and ruled part of Spain in the early Middle Ages. They were followers of Islam.

Metalwork

Craftworkers used many different metals and ways of working to decorate houses and churches. Patterns in iron, called wrought iron, decorated doors and chests. Bronze was popular for candlesticks and crosses in churches, and was sometimes used to make larger objects such as doors.

Some craftworkers were skilled at gilding paintings, sculptures and carvings.

Frescoes

Frescoes are pictures painted directly on to wet plaster. As the plaster on the wall or ceiling dries, the paint sets into clear, bright colours. Italian artists created some of the most beautiful frescoes, which can still be seen in churches and public buildings in Italy.

▲ An Italian sculptor, Lorenzo Ghiberti, made these huge bronze doors for the Baptistery in Florence. The sculptures on the doors show scenes from the Bible. They took almost 50 years to make, and were finished in 1452.

Mosaics

Thousands of tiny pieces of coloured stone or tile make up patterns and pictures called mosaics. They were often used to decorate houses and churches.

The mosaics in St Mark's church, Venice, cover the floors, walls and ceilings. They took more than 200 years to complete.

▶ These tiles and carvings are in the Alhambra, a palace built by the Moors near Granada in Spain. The carved writing is in Arabic, the language of the Moors and other peoples from North Africa.

CLOTHES AND JEWELLERY

▲ This is part of a fresco painted in about 1400. You can see the workers harvesting corn. The women are wearing kirtles, while the men wear smocks and leggings.

The clothes that people wore in the Middle Ages were very different from the clothes that we wear today. The materials were much coarser and there were fewer colours.

Workers' clothes were simple in shape and style. Women and girls wore a shapeless dress or **kirtle**, with wide sleeves. Men and boys wore leggings or trousers and a smock or tunic. The materials were mostly wool and linen.

Both women and men wore hoods and capes or lengths of material wrapped around them in cold weather. Adults often cut down their old clothes to make clothes for children.

Fashions changed slowly and only rich people could afford to follow them. As travellers brought news of different styles, wealthy people began to wear more fitted clothes. Women's dresses had tight sleeves and bodices and sometimes women wore a sleeveless coat, called a surcoat, over them. One fashion was for long trains trailing behind the dresses.

▼ A detail from a fresco of Siena, Italy, shows how nobles and their servants dressed in the early fourteenth century.

▲ These nobles are out riding, in about 1400. The women are riding side-saddle because of their long dresses.

In the later Middle Ages, women's dresses had wide, stiff sleeves and a stiff, starched collar or ruff. Men wore ruffs too. Their jackets and short trousers were padded and embroidered. Women supported their wide skirts with padding called a farthingale. Men and women wore coloured silks and velvets.

Headdresses

By the 1400s, women wore stiff, shaped headdresses instead of the simple veils of earlier times. In Italy, jewelled caps were popular, and bands which kept women's plaited hair in place. In France, women covered their hair with a cloth called a wimple, which fastened under the chin. Noblewomen wore a cone-shaped hat with a veil, called a hennin. Men wore caps or hats with feathers and jewels in them.

▲ Nobles wore rich, brightly coloured clothes and elaborate hats and caps when they went hunting. This detail is from a French tapestry made in about 1440.

Laws about dress

Noble people wore fine clothes and jewellery to show their rank. When many merchants became rich as a result of increasing trade, they showed their new wealth by wearing clothes like the nobles.

The nobles thought that this was a threat to their position. They passed laws to stop the merchants from dressing in the same style as the nobles. However, many people ignored the laws.

◄ This print shows William Caxton presenting a book to the Queen of England in about 1477. She and the noblewomen of the court are wearing hennin headdresses. The long pointed shoes were very fashionable. The shoes were called crackowes because the style came from Krakow in Poland.

Fashions for men and boys

During the 1300s, rich men wore a short, tight-fitting tunic under a long-sleeved coat or cotehardie. Sometimes the cotehardie had a badge or pattern on it, and later on the sleeves were cut in a zigzag, or dagged, shape. The coat could be trimmed with fur, or made of expensive material such as silk or **damask**.

Men and boys also wore brightly coloured trousers, called hose. Sometimes there was a different colour for each leg!

Around the beginning of the 1500s, men's fashions changed. Wealthy men now wore short, padded tunics, or doublets, with a waistcoat and a fur-lined longcoat. Soon, elaborate, puffed sleeves were worn, which could be removed.

▲ These wealthy French noblemen are wearing clothes made from expensive fabrics, richly embroidered with gold. Some are wearing fur hats. The picture comes from an illuminated manuscript made early in the fifteenth century.

▶ This farmworker is wearing simply shaped clothes, with no decoration. They are made from coarse, tough cloth. Peasants did not follow fashion. Their style of clothes stayed the same for hundreds of years.

◀ In this detail, from a fifteenth century manuscript, Italian merchants, traders and shopkeepers wear cotehardies. The customer on the left wears a short tunic and brightly coloured hose.

▲ King Henry VIII of England is wearing a style of hat that became very fashionable in the 1500s. His padded tunic and long coat are richly decorated with gold thread. Will Somers, Henry's jester, is wearing much plainer clothes.

The special clothes and hats which town mayors wear in England today are very like the styles of the 1500s.

◀ Nicholas Hilliard painted many miniatures of English nobles. This portrait of a young man shows his embroidered cloak, and short jewelled doublet. He wears a lace ruff around his neck.

Armour

In the 1100s, knights wore metal helmets and **chainmail** in battle. However, chainmail could not protect the knight completely from weapons such as arrows. The armourers, who were very skilled craftworkers, began to invent new types of armour.

The new armour was made of very strong iron and steel. There were metal plates which fitted around the knight's body and were held in place with leather straps.

▲ The Italian, Vittore Carpaccio, painted this picture in 1510. The young knight in the foreground is wearing full body armour.

Jewellery

Nobles and other wealthy people wore jewellery to show how rich and important they were. Men and women wore earrings, rings, brooches and necklaces made of gold and often set with many jewels. Wealthy people also had precious stones embroidered into their clothes and hats.

As with other crafts, styles of jewellery changed over time. In the later Middle Ages, gold jewellery from Florence, Italy, became very popular. Many goldsmiths had workshops on a bridge over the River Arno, in the middle of Florence. Today jewellery is sold from shops on the same bridge.

▼ The head in the middle of this gold brooch was carved from a precious stone that had two layers. The brown layer has been carved to show a little of the white layer. This kind of carving is called a cameo. It was made in Italy during the fourteenth century.

▲ Maria de Medici came from one of the richest and most powerful families in Italy. This portrait of her as a young girl was painted by Allori. The painting shows her wealth – the gold jewellery, the pearls and the richly embroidered clothes. Later, Maria became Queen of France.

Rings

Rings were popular in Italy during the 1300s. Women and men wore as many as they could afford, on every finger. A merchant who lived in Prato, Italy, at this time, made a list of his rings:

'... 1 big pearl on a plain gold ring, costing 40 florins. 2 sapphires, one red [a ruby], one blue, on a gold ring, costing 50 florins. 1 green emerald with chiselled gold ring, costing 10 florins. 1 blue sapphire with gold ring, given by Niccolo di Buonaccorso, cost 10 florins. 2 plain gold bands, with which she [his wife] was married, cost 8 florins for the two ...'

Heraldry

From the 1100s onwards, knights decorated their shields with strong patterns in bright colours. These **heraldic designs** helped soldiers to recognize friends and enemies across a battlefield.

The designs were also called 'coats of arms' because the knights wore them on their surcoats. This sleeveless overcoat or cloak protected the knight's armour.

The coat of arms was also embroidered on a small flag called a pennon, which flew from the knight's lance.

▲ Queen Elizabeth I of England wore magnificent jewellery and dresses. This miniature of her was painted by Nicholas Hilliard.

▶ Crosses, stripes, lions, diamonds, flowers and crescents were among the heraldic designs to be seen at the battle between France and England at Agincourt in the fifteenth century.

FESTIVALS AND HOLIDAYS

Craftworkers had to work very long hours. They began work at dawn and finished at nightfall. However there were holidays and festivals throughout the year when very few people worked. Most festivals were religious but some were held to celebrate special events, such as the marriage of a ruler.

Special days

There were about 50 special religious or holy days on which people did not work. There were three types of holy day. The first was Sunday, when nobody worked. The second was for everyone except those

▲ Musicians play woodwind instruments while young people hold hands and dance in the street. This detail comes from an Italian tapestry.

who were ploughing the fields. On a third type of holy day, all work was done except housework!

▶ The Flemish artist, Pieter Brueghel painted this picture called *A Country Feast and Dancing*, in the sixteenth century. He came from a family of artists who liked to paint ordinary people.

The ways in which people celebrated festivals changed very little over hundreds of years. In the sixteenth century the opportunity to eat plenty of food and to dance were still the most enjoyable parts of a festival for country people.

Mystery plays

In the 1300s and 1400s, craftworkers in many towns in Europe performed **mystery** plays for special occasions. Each craft guild acted out a different story from the Bible. Often the guild chose a story to link with its own trade. In York, the shipbuilders chose the story of Noah and his boat, or ark.

The players used carts or wagons in the marketplace for a stage. Usually the plays were performed on a holy day in the summer. In some towns the best play won a prize.

▲ This fresco shows a festival in a palace garden at Valfonda, Italy. The festival was held to celebrate the marriage of Maria de Medici to King Henry IV of France.

Pilgrimages

In the Middle Ages, many people travelled to holy places, or **shrines**. These were places where saints had lived, or where **miracles** had happened. Sick people hoped that they might get well if they visited shrines. Someone who made a special journey like this was called a pilgrim, and the journey was called a pilgrimage.

Some pilgrims travelled across Europe to the Holy Land, or to Santiago de Compostela in Spain or to Rome in Italy. Although the journeys were for serious purposes, for many pilgrims they were holidays as well.

Monks always wore special clothes. Their long gown, called a habit, was tied with a simple rope belt, and they wore a hooded cloak. They shaved the hair from the top of their head, in a style called a tonsure.

Sometimes monks who went on pilgrimages wore very uncomfortable clothes and no shoes. They did this to show they were sorry, or repented, for the wrong things they had done.

◀ These pages from an illuminated manuscript made in about 1500, show monks on their way to St Peter's Church in Rome.

The Age of Chivalry

The time from about 1000 to about 1400 was called the 'Age of Chivalry'. Knights were called *chevalerie* from a French word meaning a horseman. It was a great honour to become a knight. After training for a long time, a young nobleman had to show that he was honest and honourable. He swore to do his duty and to serve his lord and his ruler faithfully.

Tournaments

In order to encourage the knights and to give them some practice in the skills of fighting, lords held meetings, or tournaments, where knights gathered to show their skills. They fought in mock battles and in one-to-one, single combat. The ladies of the court presented prizes to the winners.

The knights used their lances in contests called jousting. Sometimes knights were hurt or even killed in these tournaments.

▲ Prince Henry of Breslau has just won the tournament. He is presented with a prize by the ladies of the court. The drawing comes from an early fourteenth century manuscript, made in Germany.

▼ This drawing from an Italian **medieval** Bible, shows knights jousting at a tournament.

▲ Trumpeters play from the minstrel's gallery, while the lady of the manor and her guests are served with their dinner.

Feasts

A feast at a castle or manor house was a great occasion. Perhaps the lord had returned from a crusade, or the ruler was visiting. All the guests wore their very best clothes and jewels. They were entertained as they ate an enormous meal. Sometimes there were jugglers and acrobats, or there was a play to watch. There was often music and dancing at feasts.

Minstrels and troubadours

Musicians, or minstrels, travelled around the country, playing at special feasts and other events. These minstrels were very skilled. They played horns and trumpets, harps and **lutes**. They sang stories in songs, called ballads.

Poems about adventures and about love were very popular at the courts in France, Italy and Spain between the 1100s and the 1300s. Young poets, called troubadours, entertained the nobles with these long poems and sang love songs. Often, the troubadours were also princes or nobles.

The King's minstrel

Great lords and rulers sometimes kept a group, or troupe, of minstrels who were especially skilled. One story is told about a famous minstrel called Blondel. An English king was imprisoned in a castle somewhere in Austria. Blondel wandered around the outside of many castles, singing a special song that he and the king had made up together. One day he heard the song being sung from inside a castle, in reply to him. Blondel knew that, at last, he had found the king.

▼ Adenet, 'king of the minstrels' entertains two noble ladies in this drawing from a French thirteenth century manuscript.

Dressing in the medieval style

Most people dressed very simply in the Middle Ages. Children wore the same style of clothes as their parents. Girls wore a dress, or kirtle. Boys wore a tunic, or smock, and leggings.

You will need: one sheet or large piece of material • a scarf • leggings (or trousers).

To make a kirtle:

1.   Cut a hole in the middle of the material. Make it just large enough to fit your head through.

2.   Put the material over your head.

3.   Tie the scarf around your waist to make a belt.

To make a tunic:

1.   Cut a strip off the material or sheet, about as wide as your shoulders and about as long as your height.

2.   Cut a hole in the middle of the strip of material. Make it just large enough to fit your head through.

3.   Put the cloth over your head so that it covers your front and back.

4.   Tie the scarf around your waist to make a belt.

5.   Put on your leggings (or trousers).

Jewellery

Most poor people had no decorations on their clothes. Rich people wore lots of jewellery to show their wealth and importance. Make a chain for yourself.

You will need: paper • tinfoil • glue.

1.   Glue tinfoil to each side of a piece of paper, covering the whole piece. Cut it in to small strips.

2.   Glue the ends of one strip together to make a link.

3.   Thread another strip through the first link and glue the ends together to make a second link.

4.   Carry on adding links until your chain is long enough to go around your neck and as far as your chest.

Medieval entertainers

Form a group with friends to put on a show in medieval style, or entertain your family and friends by yourself. Dress in the medieval costume you have made. Here are some of the things you could do.

1.   Choose a poem you like or make one up. Learn it by heart and practise saying it out loud. You could choose some music, played on a stringed instrument, to accompany your poem.

2.   Put on a variety show. Ask each friend with a special skill to practise for a performance which will last only for a few minutes. You could have a juggler, a singer, a joke teller or jester, a musician, a poet or storyteller, and dancers. Make sure each performance is different and that it doesn't last too long. Choose the order for the entertainers and practise introducing them, before you put on the show.

3.   Choose some music that you or your friends can play on woodwind, brass or stringed instruments. If you choose music with a strong rhythm, you could dance to the music as well.

A coat of arms

Noble families had their own coat of arms. The royal family of England had a design with a lion on it. The French nobles wore a flower design called a *fleur de lis*. The crusaders wore a cross on their tunics, to show that they were fighting for the Church.

You could make your own coat of arms. Choose your favourite colours or patterns when you design your coat of arms. You could draw something that you like or that is important to you, as well as a pattern.

You will need: paper or cardboard • colouring pens or paint • scissors • sticky tape.

1. Draw your design on the paper or card and colour it in.

2. When the design is dry, cut it out.

3. Stick it on to your clothes with sticky tape.

A pilgrim's badge

Pilgrims also wore special badges to show that they were on pilgrimage. The pilgrims who travelled to Santiago de Compostela in Spain, to the shrine of St James, had a badge which looked like a small scallop shell. It was made of clay or pewter. This scallop is still called a *coquille St Jacques*, or 'St James's shell'.

You will need: modelling clay • paint • safety pins • sticky tape.

1. Make the clay into the shape of a shell or any other shape you like. Make it quite thin, so that it isn't too heavy.

2. When the clay has hardened, paint your badge.

3. When the paint is dry, tape a safety pin to the back of the badge. Now your badge is ready to wear.

An illuminated manuscript

You can make your own illuminated manuscript, like those the monks and nuns made in the Middle Ages. Remember that they often drew pictures which showed the people and animals in the story or poem.

You will need: a pencil • colouring pencils or pens • a ruler • a gold pen • a black writing pen • paper.

1. Find a poem, or short story that you like. You could make up your own, or copy something from a book.

2. Use a ruler to measure a margin about two or three centimetres inside the edges of the paper. This will make a frame so that you write inside this area.

3. Draw the frame in gold.

4. Use your pencil to sketch out how things will fit inside the frame. Allow space for a big box at the beginning of your poem or story. This is for the first letter of the first word.

5. When you are happy with your sketch, draw the box with gold pen. Also in gold, write the first letter, very big, inside the box.

6. Use your colours to draw patterns or a picture inside the box around the letter.

7. Write out the rest of the poem or story with a black writing pen. You could read your poem or story to your family or friends.

GLOSSARY

apprentice: Someone who is learning a trade.

Black Death: A plague which killed 25 million people in Europe in the 1300s. It was spread by fleas on rats.

blacksmith: A blacksmith used hot iron to make and mend all types of tools and weapons. The iron was heated in a very hot fire and then shaped on a metal block, called an anvil. As the iron cooled, it set hard.

chainmail: Armour made of linked rings, or chains, of metal.

Christian: A follower of the teachings of Jesus Christ.

convent: The place where nuns live and work. In the Middle Ages some convents were governed by an abbot or an abbess and were called abbeys. They often included a church and farmland.

court: A gathering of a ruler and nobles, or the place where they met.

Crusades: Journeys to fight the Turks for possession of the Holy Land. There were six Crusades between 1096 and 1303.

damask: Cloth that has a woven pattern, first made in Damascus in Syria.

distaff: A stick which holds wool or flax while spinning.

fibres: Strong, thread-like parts of a plant.

fresco: A picture painted on to damp plaster.

gilding: Putting a thin layer of gold on to something.

guilds: Organizations of craftworkers.

heraldic designs: The special patterns which made up a coat of arms.

illuminated: Decorated or illustrated with patterns and pictures.

Islam: A religion started by Muhammad in AD622. Its followers are called Muslims.

kirtle: A long, loose gown. Later, an outer petticoat.

knights: Soldiers on horseback who fought for a ruler. Horses and armour were expensive, so knighthood became an honour for rich men.

loom: A wooden frame for weaving cloth.

lute: A musical instrument with strings.

manor: The land belonging to a noble family.

manuscripts: Books written by hand, usually before printing was invented. The word comes from two latin words, 'manus' which means hand and 'scriptus' which means written.

medieval: From the Middle Ages.

merchants: Traders, people who bought and sold goods.

minted: Made. The place where coins were made was called a mint.

miracle: An event which cannot be explained.

monastery: The place where monks live and work. In the Middle Ages some monasteries had large amounts of land, which the monks farmed.

monks: Men who give their lives to serving God. They pray and hold several church services every day. In the Middle Ages they were teachers and farmers. Monks do not marry.

Moors: People who lived in North Africa. The Moors ruled in Spain from AD711-1492.

moulds: Hollow forms which shape materials such as clay, plaster, metal or glass.

mystery: The word 'mystery' here comes from *mestier*, a word like the French *metier* which means a trade. It also means something which cannot be explained. The mystery plays were sometimes called miracle plays.

nobles: The most important people in the country, after the ruler's family. They held important positions at court, and were usually very rich.

nuns: Women who give their lives to serving God and who do not marry. In the Middle Ages, nuns taught, farmed and made tapestries.

peasants: Land workers.

Pope: In the early Middle Ages, there was one Christian Church. It was called 'catholic' which means general or universal. The Pope, who lived mostly in Rome, was the head of the Church. Later, other churches were formed. Today, the Pope heads the Roman Catholic Church.

Renaissance: The time from about 1400 to about 1600 when people's interest in the ideas, art and architecture of ancient Greece and Rome was 'reborn'.

shrines: Places where people remember holy people or saints.

silk: A thread made by silkworm caterpillars, and woven into soft cloth.

spices: Dried plant seeds, roots or leaves, such as ginger, pepper and nutmeg. Spices were very expensive in the Middle Ages.

spindle: A pin or rod, usually made from wood, which turns or winds thread when it is being spun.

Further reading

Costume and Clothes, Penelope Paul, 'Legacies' series (Wayland Publishers Ltd., 1995)
Food & Feasts in the Middle Ages, Imogen Dawson, 'Food & Feasts' series (Wayland Publishers Ltd., 1994)
The Late Middle Ages, Brian Williams (ed.), 'History of the World' series (Cherrytree Press Ltd., 1995)
Over 450 years ago: In the New World, Philip Sauvain, 'History Detective' series (Zoë Books Ltd., 1993)
The Renaissance, Tim Wood, 'See through History' series (Heinemann Children's Reference, 1995)
Wonders of the Medieval World, Neil Morris, 'Wonders of the World' series (Belitha Press Ltd., 1995)

INDEX